REFLECTIONS

Isolene Scarborough

REFLECTIONS:

FEELINGS OF THE HEART

By

Isolene Scarborough

With

Prayer Journal by PraiseLinks

Editing, Design, Publishing

by Joy Carter for *Just Get It Write*, a division of

PraiseLinks

2014

First Printing: 2014

ISBN 978-1-312-13351-8

Ordering Information:

Special discounts are available on quantity purchases by churches, groups, businesses, educators, and others. For details, contact the publisher at the above listed address.

U.S. trade bookstores and wholesalers:

Please contact Ms. Scarborough via email: isodarlene@gmail.com

Dedication

To my Lord and Savior Jesus Christ...

Thank you for your wisdom and inspiration.
Without you I am nothing.

To my Mom, Ms. Fannie Scober...
You gave me the wisdom and knowledge to make it to this place in my life. This book I give to you from my heart to let you know how much I love you and appreciate your prayers and support.

To Darlene...
Thank you for your constant support,
patience, and encouragement.
I would have never achieved this dream without your help.

To William Manuel Branch...
I dedicate this book to you for everything we've been through together, and for all the lessons learned along the way.

TO GOD BE THE GLORY!

Table of Contents

Reflections

My Children and What You Are To Me

You're the apple of my eyes.
You're the love of my heart.
You're the joy of my life.
You're my inspiration of God
You're the smile upon my face.
You're my tears that fall from heaven.
You're the pain in my side.
You're my army of defeat.
You're my light that shines through the day.
You're my stars that sparkle in the Night.
You're my breeze in the middle of the heat.
You're my warmth in the midst of the cold.

DRUGS

Drugs are a substance that damages the brain and the blood cells; it moves like a box of chocolate moving this way and that way, never knowing which part of the body it's going to attack next. Like a butterfly flying from flower to flower and limb to limb, never knowing where it's going to perch next. Drugs flow through the tunnel of blood cells taking one disease after another, like the water flowing down the river. We're too up, we're too down to even realize or understand the symptoms and side effects that drugs do to our body, because we're too busy taking it, using it eating it, chewing it, drinking it, smoking it, dipping it, stealing it, selling it, buying it, shooting it up, wasting it, misunderstanding it, and abusing it to even know what drugs are really doing to our health, because we don't understand nor do we want to understand the true meaning of drugs.

PEACE

Peace is the way of the world, that fall short of hope, driving through the city of temptation, stopping at the light of lust, crashing in the road of redemption, riding to the hospital of admonition, laying in the bed of sin, sleeping through the pain of weakness, looking in the eyes of the devil praying and wishing for another chance, missing the door of Heaven, falling down the elevator of integration, landing on the ground of salvation, walking through the streets of kindness, looking down the path of some grace running down the road for some mercy, skipping on the grass of love, falling on the dew of faith-less, rolling over the dirt of misery, struggling for forgiveness sittings on the rock of patience, crying at the mess you made of your life.

MAMA HOOPER

Mama Hooper...

you're like a tree planted by the river,

overlooking the view of fear,

sitting by the bank of the river,

talking on the phone of gossip,

listening to the radio of temptation,

changing the station of sin,

clapping to the beat of grace,

stomping to the rhythm of mercy,

dipping in the river of the Jordan,

looking at the stars of hope,

glazing the moon of hopefulness,

dancing on the clouds of joy,

chasing the rainbow of integration,

falling down the rain of kindness,
fighting the war of destruction,
praying and wishing for peace,
glaring in the eyes of God,
mixing and matching on the grounds of happiness, walking on the path of redemption,
picking the flower of colors,
tasting the sweet of honey,
teaching the word of truth,
opening the eyes of the world,
looking toward the promise land,
falling in the arms of Jesus,
making Him your final rest place.

JESUS

Jesus is the most powerful man of the world. He sits high and looks low; He knows our every need and want. Jesus fills us with His love, spirit, wisdom, knowledge and power to be or become anybody we want to be.

We're too busy to see or know who Jesus really is, because we're too busy getting in each other's business, cheating, fighting, lying, stealing, blaming, looking at each other faults, smoking dope, drinking and having a pity party with our self to even know that Jesus is the way and the answer.

Have your ever taken the time out to put yourself in Jesus' place and go through all that He went through for us? "NO". You see Jesus was ridiculed, he was spit on, beaten to the tearing of His flesh, and died on the cross for our sins and the most important thing is what Jesus was beaten with. How many of us could have gone through all what Jesus went through? None of us could go through all that Jesus went through. He never complained about a thing, he took it a like a true man.

We could never go through what Jesus went through because we are too busy complaining about this and that, and what we have and don't have.

If you really look at, it we don't have anything. Everything we got belongs to Jesus, nothing we have is ours. He just let us borrow it for a little while we are here, and if we can quit fighting one another, stabbing each other in the back and talking about one another, then we can see Jesus for who he really is.

I thank Jesus for myself as well as for others. He woke us up this morning and that is a lot to be thankful for, because some didn't wake up this morning. Each day God wakes us up is a blessing in the sky; to see a new day is more than any of us can ask for.

Also I thank God for last night's sleep and waking me up to a bright new day in Jesus Christ. If we take the time to know and love Jesus for who He really is in our life and to honor and glorify His name, we will be amazed at what He will do for us.

LIFE

Life is like a ship without a sail that travels through the winds of love, disappointment, trials and tribulations. Life sits high above the hills of revelation, wondering how to get down the path of salvation onto the streets of hope, traveling this way and that way, never knowing which way it's going.

Until you run into the city of hell, falling down in the battle of redemption, wasting away along the wayside, falling down the water fall of admonition, skipping down the rollercoaster of mercy, trying to get to grace, shouting along the river of joy, to the land of peace and falling short of the glory, into the ocean of sin, praying and hoping that God will hear your cry and bring you through the wave of love into those arms of His.

DARLENE

Darlene you're like a bee, flying from flower to flower, taking the sweets of the flower from this place to that place, falling on the grounds of honey, tasting the sweetness of love, mixing and matching in the winds of danger, fighting the battle of destruction, chasing the petal of redemption, walking in the breezes of hope-full-ness, looking to the sun of hope, glazing in the stars of mercy, glaring at the moon of grace, wishing and praying for a miracle, crying to the tone of gossip, turning the station of pain, listening to the singing of angels.

Shouting to the beat of joy, kneeling a the river of Jordan, laying hands in the ocean of tears, dipping in the river of peace, looking in the eyes of Jesus, pushing your way through the promised land, reaching for the hands of God, holding onto the arms of faith.

He's holding you on the right and I 'm holding you on the left; we're taking you through the Promised Land, right into the land of freedom… the final resting place.

ASHLEY

You're the love of your mother's heart

You're the tears of a mother's joy.

You're the rain that fall from Heaven.

You're the sun that glazing in the day.

You're the moon that brightens up the night.

You're the stars that glitters in the sky

You're the wind that blows across the ocean.

You're the water that dances over the wave.

You're the breeze that shakes among the leaves.

You're the sweet-ness of your father's heart.

You're the apple of Jesus eyes.

TEMPTATION

Temptation is the way of lust,
that fills the body with sin,
making it way through the field of adultery,
moving down the river of seeking,
trying to find the way back to hope,
forgetting the road to salvation,
turning down the path off convent,
paddling the ocean of confession,
jumping the wave of forgiveness,
grabbing the arms of hope,
looking to the hills of peace,
wishing for a ride to Heaven,
listening to the voice of the devil and
falling in the arms of fornication,
looking in the eyes of God,
praying for mercy,
losing the battle of forgiveness,
laying in your mess of sin;
trying to get to the golden gate, you fell on the nail of
faith, now you are walking with no way out.

HATE

Hate is the way of sin that fall short of love, running through the jungle of destruction, falling down the water fall of evil, wondering for some integration, looking by the wayside of Satan wishing and praying for some peace. Overlooking the ride of hope, sliding through the wave of hell, fighting for your way out, knocking over the post of Heaven, falling in the pits of hell, trying to dig your way to forgiveness, missing the path of kindness, landing in the middle of lust, feeling your way through frustration screaming and yelling for some understanding, waiting for some patience, skipping and hoping across the grass of salvation, strolling down the side walk of lying trying to get to the other side the truth listening to radio of gossip, never knowing the fact, dashing and dogged your true feeling on the inside, missing the opportunity to make it, thinking you're sitting on the road of happiness, laying in a bed of nails, looking in the eyes of Jezebel made hell your final destination.

THE DEVIL

The Devil is the way of sin, the rumble, the streets of evil, chasing the flower of lust, going from flower to flower tasting the sweets of Jezebel, landing in the arms of temptation, running through the fire of hell, dancing and screaming for some water, praying and hoping for help, walking on the dew of adultery, sliding on the grounds of danger, looking for the sign of love, skipping down the road of Heaven, thinking you've made it in, overlooking the sigh of truth, lying your way through faith, wondering how to get the pat of salvation, falling in the vibe of damnation, paddling the ocean of integration, skiing the wave of meekness, falling in the ocean of death, crying and yelling for peace, missing the mark of God washing down the water of kindness, into the barrel of destruction, cracking the ground of peace, leaping over the hole of grace, landing in the middle of sex, trying to find your way out making a mess of your situation.

JEALOUSY

Jealousy is the path of the devil, creeping through the jungle of evil shooting at the limb of honesty, falling short of love, hitting the bark of sin, bouncing off the tree of kindness, landing on the bushes of temptation skipping and hopping on the grounds of adultery, looking to see who is watching, wishing and praying for gates to open so you can step right on in- missing the trap of patience, chasing the deer of trials and tribulations, fighting for the life of joy, stumbling on the truth of meekness, waiting for grace to pick you up, never knowing where it is going to take you, like a box of chocolate hitting this and hitting that; never knowing what you're going to hit next, looking for mercy, laying in the heat of passion, looking in the eyes of hell.

JOY

Joy is the way of the heart, rolling down the roller-coaster of happiness, looping through the ride of faith, wishing and praying for a miracle hanging on the edge of temptation, missing the boat of friendship, wrestling with your fear, struggling for some communication, because you're listening to the line of gossip, dipping in the hands of truth, losing the battle of righteousness and fighting for some understanding; looking for a ride to Heaven, staggering on the road of hope, falling on the ground of meekness, hoping for a sign of peace, looking for salvation because you ran out of grace into the bed of hopefulness, dreaming for rolls of promises, ending in the gates of lying, losing the fight of kindness, to the battle of cheating because you never sang the song of deliverance.

SIN

Sin is the way of the world, that travels through the jungle of lust, wing from tree to tree of adoration, hanging on the limbs of integration, slipping down the bark of hell, wishing and praying for the river of salvation, while padding the creeks of death, looking for the path of hope, singing and shouting for joy, falling down the cliff of faithfulness into the bay of mercy, wasting on the way of grace, dipping I n the sand of peace, trying to get to the other side of hell, praying for the doors of Heaven to open and push you right on in, on the way up you fall in the hands of the devil, because you slip and slide your whole life through…

SALVATION

Salvation is the way of PEACE that pushes its way through the road of happiness, creeping along the way of forgiveness, right past the city of kindness into the show of love...

Waddling down the sidewalk of hope, skipping and hopping on the grass of faithfulness and rolling down the path faith; looking for the sign of meekness and falling short of temptation into the arms of revolution and over the hills of confidence.

Falling on the edge of seeking, crying and praying for Glory, while lying on the bed of promise and dreaming, on the way to Heaven and looking in the eyes of God, singing and shouting for joy...

... thinking you had the world, listening to adultery and slipping on the gates of lust, falling short of righteousness, missing the promise of God, cheating yourself to sin and missing your destination.

HEAVEN

Heaven is the root of happiness that falls short of hope, running into the gates of Hell, screaming and crying for forgiveness, trying to get to faithfulness, looking down the path of salvation, skipping and hopping on the road to integrity...

While walking the grass of gentleness, reaching for the bark of kindness, falling down the hills of fornication into the ocean of adultery.

Sliding down the waterfall for cheating, on the wave of admonition, into the sea of jealousy, missing your turn to Heaven, crying and praying for the opportunity to make it in, missing the road up, while running from the way of Peace, falling on the sign of Hell, looking and searching for a way out, missed the door in front of you, looking in the eyes of the devil....your final resting place.

HOPE

Hope is the life of the world, that rumble the town of provision and jumping on the saddle of meekness, while searching the road of peace and galloping down the path of seeking, looking for the sign of truth. Falling on the ground of lust, trying to get to the stage of faithfulness, while singing the songs of joy, dipped in the river of rightness, walking through the creek of darkness, looping the tree of kindness, slipping in the water of faith, praying for forgiveness, hoping God will hear your cry and bring you out of the ditch of Hell stomping the mud of sin, wishing for a ride to mercy, looking for a bout of confidence, creeping through the field of grace, fumbling and sliding on the wheat of salvation, missing the hands of God, lying your way through the corn of promises, never made it to the end, hoping and praying for a new beginning.

Reflections

7 DAY PRAYER JOURNAL

As you reflect on the words of the passages in this book, allow God to minister to your heart and soul. The following pages are included for your use as a personal prayer journal for you to draw closer to God. Each day includes a short devotional based on one of the passages in this book, plus a scripture reference and room to write notes as you grow stronger in your faith and in your walk with God.

Our Father loves you. He wants nothing more than to commune with, talk with, comfort and be at peace with you. The point of this book was to show how easily we can slip off the path of righteousness and into trouble when we allow ourselves to lose or compromise our connection to Him.

The "PRAYER POINTS" are only meant to give you suggested areas to pray over. Use them as a simple starting point to begin a daily session of prayer with the Lord, but pray from your own heart, with your own words...there is no wrong way to pray, so use this time to develop your own distinct manner of communication with God. He's there to listen and He will make His presence known if you allow space for Him to speak back to you during your times of prayer, reflection and devotion.

Take the time to use this journal. Take the time to reflect on the pieces in this book and the scriptures in the journal pages. Then take the time to pray. When you reflect on how much you really need God and how much He really loves you, you will discover such a wellspring of Peace, Joy and Happiness that you won't ever want to move through life without it again.

READ. REFLECT. PRAY AND BE BLESSED!

DAY 1: MY CHILDREN

Scripture: Psalm 127:3-5

Reflection: If you are a parent, you have hopefully experienced the undeniable bond between you and your child. The Bible tells us that children are a blessing from God, a reward and even a resource to us as parents.
If you have not experienced having children in the literal physical sense, take heart because there are many people in whom God has placed the capacity to nurture and love children and others as if they were their own.

The beauty of this parent-child relationship is that it so perfectly illustrates our relationship to God, our Father. The pride and the joy; the lessons and the growth, all of the stages children go through to get to maturity and all of the missteps along the way. Even if you feel like you are not the best parent or haven't been the best child, we can look to God's example of love and sacrifice to gain a deeper appreciation for how much we are worth and just how much we need the Lord.

Prayer Points:

- Where am I in relationship to God?
- What kind of child am I?
- Lord, help me to know and trust You as my loving Father.

NOTES:

DAY 2: PEACE

Scripture: Philippians 4:7

Reflection: What is your definition of peace? Do you have it now? Can you remember a time in your life when you did? The Word of God tells us that there is a peace which goes beyond anything we can understand, and that *THAT* peace can guard our hearts and our minds. Isn't that just amazing?

The more you spend time focused on God and developing a real relationship with Him, the more peace can manifest in your life. Ask yourself: ***Have I become so comfortable with chaos and the hustle-bustle of life that I don't even want peace?*** Only you can mine the depths of your own heart and mind to truthfully answer that question. Ask God for help in recognizing your need for God's peace.

Prayer Points:

- How is the lack of peace affecting me?
- Do I create peace or chaos for myself or even others?
- Lord, help me to know Your Peace.

NOTES:

DAY 3: GOSSIP

Scripture: Proverbs 12:18; Proverbs 15:4; James 3:8-10

Reflection: One thing that can surely wreck our peace and that of others is the words we speak. Study the selected verses and others very carefully to understand the power and gravity of what we say to ourselves, about ourselves; to and about others. Do your words speak poison, division, and death, or do your words bring health, healing and life to you and those around you? In this age of reality t.v. and instant celebrity even among the people of God, how easily has gossip become a part of your everyday conversation? Does such gossip benefit you in anyway and if so, how? Do you feel like you fit in with the crowd by participating in gossip? Would you feel bothered if you were the subject of other people's gossip? The Bible tells us that the power of life and death lies in our tongue. This is not just a reminder to speak affirmations of wealth and prosperity over our lives, but also to guard against letting our tongues become weapons of mass destruction.

Prayer Points:

- Who or what do I talk about too much or in negative ways?
- Have my words caused others harm?
- Lord, let the words of my mouth be acceptable in thy sight...

NOTES:

DAY 4: JESUS

Scripture: Isaiah 9:6

Reflection: Do you know who Jesus is? Not just who others have described Him to be, but do you really know Him for yourself? Have you allowed Him the space and opportunity to truly be *your* Wonderful Counselor, *your* Mighty God, *your* Eternal Father, or *your very own* Prince of Peace? Is your knowledge of Jesus based on head-knowledge or heart knowledge? Is He real to you and for you, and if not, do you want Him to be?

Many times we get swept up in our traditions of religion and doctrine and even church-going habits, without really seeking out or experiencing Jesus on a personal, tangible level for ourselves. What a shame! As the old hymn says, "...there are depths of love that I cannot know till I cross the narrow sea; there are heights of joy that I may not reach till I rest in peace with thee. Draw me nearer, nearer blessed Lord".
If you seek Him, you will find Him.

Prayer Points:

- Can I know Jesus for myself?
- What must I do to encounter Jesus?
- Jesus, show me how real You are...

NOTES:

DAY 5: TEMPTATION

Scripture: I. Corinthians 10:13; James 4:7

Reflection: Temptation is an inevitable part of life. All of us are or will be tempted by something or someone at some point in our lives. Let's face it, if Jesus was tempted in the wilderness, we will not be able to avoid temptation in this life. We *can*, however, triumph over it.

The Word of God lets us know that we will most certainly be tempted, but that God will not tempt us beyond our ability to choose what is right, *AND* He will always provide us with a way of escape from the temptation. In other words, we get to determine whether or not we pass the *"temptation tests"* in our lives, be they tests of fidelity in relationships, having the last word in every conversation, financial or business matters, lying to get out of a traffic ticket or cheating on our taxes. If we yield to God instead of to temptation, we can get so good at resisting temptation and passing the tests, that we'll see them coming a mile away. God's Word is our Escape!

Prayer Points:

- What areas am I most tempted in?
- Do I have the power to resist temptation?

  Lord, fill me with Your spirit so I can recognize temptations that are coming my way.

NOTES:

DAY 6: SALVATION

Scripture: Romans 1:6; Acts 4:12

Reflection: Salvation denotes rescue, deliverance, and freedom. Sin separates us from God and binds us captive to that hopeless state of separation. Did you know that you have actually been called to belong to Jesus Christ by His redeeming act of sacrifice? Salvation comes when we accept it from Him and it remains in place as we daily seek to know and serve Him more.

There are many types of rescue, such as being saved from drowning or saved from financial ruin or even from the hands of a violent mugging. ***True Salvation*** however, involves your soul and where it will spend eternity after it is freed from these mortal bodies. No one else can offer the absolute salvation that Jesus does, and there is no other way to be truly saved than by the name and blood of Jesus Christ. Won't you trust and accept His precious gift of salvation today?

Prayer Points:

- What must I do to be saved?
- How do I live a saved life??
- Lord, help me to learn and lean on You for my salvation.

NOTES:

DAY 7: HOPE & JOY

Scripture: Psalm 31:24; Romans 15:13

Reflection: What do you hope for in your heart of hearts? What brings you the most real joy? Is it a person, place or thing, or perhaps a state of being?

The word of God has much to say about hope, what we hope for, and who we should place our hope in-namely Jesus and His shed blood. It is okay to hope for things like a home or a promotion. These things can actually be a source of happiness in life, but can they bring you real joy? Romans 15:13 reveals that God is a God of hope, who has the power to fill you with "all Joy and Peace" and hope, through the Holy Spirit.

What a completely loving Savior He is if we would only believe in Him and on Him more than anything. As Jeremiah 29:11 reminds us, God has ***hopeful*** plans for us. That thought alone should bring you a measure of reassurance and joy.

Prayer Points:

- What makes me happy? What brings me joy?
- What do I hope for most?
- Lord, help me put my hope and trust in You that I may experience real Peace and Joy.

NOTES:

ADDITIONAL NOTES

About The Author

Ms. Isolene Scarborough has been applying herself to writing over the last three years, following a series of challenges in her life. She is the mother of two sons and five grandsons, and has devoted herself to missionary work for most of her life.

She resides in Sloan, NC.

www.ingramcontent.com/pod-product-compliance
Ingram Content Group UK Ltd.
Pitfield, Milton Keynes, MK11 3LW, UK
UKHW041839200726
13854UKWH00003BA/1218

9 781312 133518